THE WAY
PART 1

THE EVANGELICAL CATHOLIC
LEADER/INDIVIDUAL

Published by The Word Among Us Press

7115 Guilford Drive, Suite 100

Frederick, Maryland 21704

wau.org

23 22 21 20 19   1 2 3 4 5

ISBN: 978-1-59325-357-8

eISBN: 978-1-59325-368-4

Nihil Obstat: Msgr. Michael Morgan, J.D., J.C.L.
Censor Librorum
August 13, 2019

Imprimatur: +Most Rev. Felipe J. Estevez, S.T.D.
Diocese of St. Augustine
August 14, 2019

Cover design by Austin Franke

Interior design by Down to Earth Design

Made and printed in the United States of America

Library of Congress Control Number: 2019911772

Contents

Introduction

Follow me.
Matthew 4:19

Long ago, Jesus spoke these simple words to his disciples. Jesus speaks the same words to us today. We can hear it in the restlessness of our hearts amidst the frantic pace of modern life. We can sense it in our most honest yearnings for purpose in a world inundated with distraction. This introductory small group guide aims to echo this call: "Follow me." All of us are called to pursue "the way, and the truth, and the life" (John 14:6), which are not *some things* but rather *Someone*—the Word made flesh, God incarnated in the person of Jesus Christ.

In his first encyclical letter, *Deus Caritas Est* (God is Love), Pope Benedict XVI reminded us that "being Christian is not the result of an ethical choice or a lofty idea, but the encounter with an event, a person" (1). This person is, of course, Jesus Christ, the cornerstone of our faith and the reason for our hope. St. John Paul II proclaimed Christ "the foundation and center of history, . . . its meaning and ultimate goal" (*Novo Millennio Ineunte*, 5). This person—Jesus Christ, the center and ultimate goal of human history—is the foundation and focal point for this *The Way* study.

Our purpose here is to prompt an actual encounter with the living God—with Jesus Christ risen from the dead. In communion with the U.S. Conference of Catholic Bishops, we hope that the following small group sessions will help participants "consciously grow in the life of Christ through experience, reflection, prayer, and study" (USCCB, *Our Hearts Were*

Burning Within Us, 5).[1] In addition to a presentation of truths regarding Our Lord and his Church, *The Way* seeks to facilitate a deeply personal, yet at the same time communal, encounter with God.

We all long for deep friendship with our brothers and sisters in Christ. These types of friendships form when we can gather together to express and solidify that which bonds us for eternity—our faith and hope in God through Jesus Christ. Our common Baptism binds the Church together and makes the way for Christian community. We hope that for each reader, each participant in this exploration, *The Way* might become an avenue for truly intentional Christian community—one that reflects the manifold gifts of the body of Christ, one that nourishes real growth in each disciple of Jesus, one that responds to the call of Christ to be a light unto the world (see Matthew 5:14).

St. John Paul II promoted small Christian communities as a means of evangelization, as instruments for effectively sharing the good news of Jesus Christ in the world. Being a part of a thriving small group promotes substantial spiritual growth and even conversion, and this sort of holy vitality quite naturally spills over into the lives of others. As St. John Paul II noted, "Those who have come into genuine contact with Christ cannot keep him for themselves; they must proclaim him" (*Novo Millennio Ineunte*, 40).

Mature disciples, who are continually enlivened by their encounters with Christ, often serve as strong witnesses when it comes to sharing the gospel. Perhaps no one stands readier, with more excitement, to share the beauty of Jesus than one who continues to meet him daily. In the same way that we are

---

[1] United States Conference of Catholic Bishops, *Our Hearts Were Burning Within Us: A Pastoral Plan for Adult Faith Formation in the United States* (Washington, DC: USCCB, 1999), 5.

compelled to share good news with those around us, there is nothing more natural, after having received the ultimate "good news" (or gospel) of Jesus Christ, than to burst forth and share this great gift with the world. This sharing sits at the heart of Catholic evangelization.

It is in our continually confirmed experience that effective small groups can facilitate deep, personal encounters with God—encounters that will bear the fruit of evangelization for years to come. Small groups can help reawaken the evangelical impulse of our tradition and reposition evangelization as the "essential mission of the Church" and "her deepest identity" (Pope Paul VI, *Evangelii Nuntiandi*, 14). After a personal and life-changing encounter with Christ, we cannot help but share with others the good news.

> *Out of the abundance of the heart the mouth speaks.*
> Matthew 12:34

The content of *The Way* leads individuals and groups to reflect upon the heart and habits of discipleship. As Catholic disciples of Jesus, who find our principle encounter with the Lord in the Eucharist, "the source and summit of the Christian life" (*Catechism*, 1324), we mature to the extent that we allow the heart and habits of Jesus and his people to become ever more our own. The heart and habits of Catholic discipleship include the following fundamentals (see *General Directory for Catechesis*, 88-92):

- A life centered upon God—the Trinity—as revealed in and through Jesus and his Church

- A committed and spiritually formative sacramental and liturgical life

- A life of consistent, deep, personal, and communal prayer

- A life steeped in Scripture

- A shared communal life in the Church—the body of Christ

- A life on mission—sharing the good news of Jesus with others in word and deed

- A life of ongoing conversion and growth in freedom as we conform to Christ in our character and in the particulars of our vocations

Both parts of *The Way* reinforce all these elements of discipleship, but they each emphasize different topics to foster sequential growth and new habits. Part 1 looks at friendship with Jesus, personal prayer, and devotion to Scripture, while Part 2 delves into the Eucharist, community, ongoing conversion (including the Sacrament of Reconciliation) and mission.

We hope that this small group guide will help you further encounter Jesus Christ, the center and cornerstone of our faith, giving your life "a new horizon and a decisive direction" (*Deus Caritas Est*, 1). We pray that these studies will inspire you to place Jesus at the center of your life and help you to grow in the likeness of the One we call both Friend and Savior.

All in all, our goal through *The Way* is none other than to help you discover and rediscover that "God is love, and he who abides in love abides in God, and God abides in him" (1 John 4:16). We follow the pastoral principle that frames the whole life of the Church and all her endeavors—"Whether something is proposed for belief, for hope or for action, the love of our Lord must always be made accessible, so that anyone can see that all the works of perfect Christian virtue spring from love and have no other objective than to arrive at love" (*Cate-*

chism, 25). Our prayer is "that your love may abound more and more" (Philippians 1:9) and that your witness to Jesus Christ might plant the seeds for a "new springtime" of evangelization (St. John Paul II, *Redemptoris Missio*, 2) in the Church and throughout the world. Hear the words of Jesus today, "Follow me" (Matthew 4:19) and experience the truth that will set you free (see John 8:32).

How to Use This Guide

Welcome to *The Way*, a small group guide to help people follow Jesus of Nazareth and to help those who already follow Jesus to take the next step in their discipleship journey.

Weekly Sessions

The weekly session material includes opening and closing prayer suggestions; the Scripture and Tradition passages to be discussed that week; questions to prompt discussion, ideas or action; and suggestions to help you continue following Jesus through the week.

Unlike some small group Scripture discussion guides that progress consecutively through a book of the Bible, each session in this guide is self-contained. That way, if you or a friend attends a small group for the first time during session 3, there won't be a need to "catch up." Anyone can just dive right in with the rest of the group. Instead of building sequentially, the sessions deepen thematically, helping you follow Jesus more and more closely.

Although each session in *The Way* may stand alone, however, the topics are arranged in two-week sets. The first week introduces a theme, and the second week continues and deepens the discussion on that theme. The three sets are

(a) sessions 1 and 2 on friendship with Jesus,

(b) sessions 3 and 4 on prayer, and

(c) sessions 5 and 6 on Scripture.

The more you take notes, jot down ideas or questions, underline verses in your Bible (if you bring one to your small group, which we recommend!), and refer back to the previous sessions, the more God has the opportunity to speak to you through the discussion and the ideas he places in your heart. As with anything, the more you put in, the more you get back.

The best way to take advantage of each week's discussion is to carry the theme into your life by following the suggestions in the "Encountering Christ This Week" sections. Your small group facilitator will talk about the recommendations during each session. You will have a chance to ask questions and share experiences from previous weeks.

If you're not in a small group, *The Way* can help you follow Jesus on your own. Consider the questions asked of each Scripture passage and follow up with the suggestions in "Encountering Christ This Week."

Appendices

Helpful appendices for both participants and facilitators supplement the weekly materials. Appendices A through D are for participants, and appendices E through G are for group facilitators.

Prior to your first group meeting, please read appendix A, "Small Group Discussion Guide." These guidelines will help every person in the group set a respectful tone that creates the space for encountering Christ together. This small group will differ from other discussion groups you may have experienced. Is it a lecture? No. A book club? No. Appendix A will help you understand what this small group is and how you can help seek a Spirit-led discussion. Every member is responsible for the quality of the group dynamics. This appendix will help you fulfill your role of being a supportive and involved group member.

Appendix B is a resource to enhance and deepen your relationship with Jesus through developing a daily habit of praying with Scripture. This appendix also includes a simple outline of the prayer method *lectio divina*, or "divine reading," in which one listens to God through Scripture and enters into prayerful dialogue with the Lord. We recommend using the *lectio divina* method of prayer with each week's suggested Scripture passages found in "Encountering Christ This Week."

In appendix C, you will find a guide to ACTS, an acronym for a simple way to pray every day. Spending as little as two minutes a day on each letter of ACTS is one of the simplest ways to grow in prayer.

In appendix D, you will find a guide to the Sacrament of Reconciliation, commonly known as Confession. This sacrament bridges the distance we might feel from God that results from a variety of causes, including unrepented sin. If you want to grow closer to Jesus and experience great peace, the Sacrament of Reconciliation provides a fast track. This appendix will help alleviate any anxiety by leading you through the steps of preparing for and going to Confession.

While appendices A through D are for small group participants and facilitators alike, appendices E through G assist the facilitators in their role. A facilitator is not a teacher. His or her role is to buoy the conversation, encourage fruitful group discussion, and tend to the group dynamics.

Appendix E provides guidance and best practices for facilitating a small group successfully and includes recommendations for any difficult group dynamics that could arise. You will find guidelines on what makes a group work: building genuine friendships, calling for the Holy Spirit to be the group's true facilitator, and seeking joy together.

Appendix F takes the facilitator from the general to the specific, providing detailed leader notes for each session of *The Way*. Read those notes four or five days before each group meeting. The notes will help you prepare each session by providing a "heads up" on the content and issues that pertain to discussing these particular Scripture passages.

Facilitators should read appendix G well in advance of the first meeting. It has the guidance you need to lead prayer and encourage prayer by group members. While the material in each session includes a suggested prayer, this is only support material. It's far better spiritually for the group to pray in their own words. Appendix F guides the facilitator on how to help that happen.

Learning this skill is important. It will model for the group members how to talk to Jesus in their own words. Closing with extemporaneous prayer seals the time you have spent together by offering up the discoveries, questions, and joys of your conversation. Appendix G will help you guide your group from awkward beginnings to a deepening experience of talking to God.

Appendix G will also help the facilitator bring the "Encountering Christ This Week" section into the weekly discussion. It provides concrete suggestions on how to encourage and support group members in their personal engagement with the topics discussed. The facilitator plays a key role in helping participants allow Jesus to become more and more the center of their lives.

Enjoy the adventure!

Friendship with Jesus

I have called you friends.
John 15:15

Opening Prayer

Read the following prayer by St. Anselm of Canterbury (1033–1109):

> O Lord, our God,
> teach our hearts this day where and how to see you,
> where and how to find you.
>
> You have made us and remade us,
> and you have bestowed on us
> all the good things we possess,
> and still we do not know you.
>
> We have not yet done that
> for which we were made.
>
> Teach us to seek you,
> for we cannot seek you

unless you teach us,
or find you
unless you show yourself to us.

Let us seek you in our desire;
Let us desire you in our seeking.
Let us find you by loving you;
Let us love you when we find you.[2]

We pray through Jesus Christ, Our Lord. Amen.

Sharing Our Experience

Take a couple of minutes to turn to a partner and tell them about a close friend. Use the following questions as loose guidelines for your conversation.

1. What is your friend like?

2. What first attracted you to your friend?

3. How do you spend time together?

4. Talk about your conversations—why are they so good/interesting?

5. What makes your friendship solid?

6. What habits do you need in order to cultivate your friendship?

7. How have you changed since you met your friend?

8. What could endanger your friendship?

---

[2] Adapted into plural from Jacquelyn Lindsey, ed., *Catholic Prayers for All Occasions* (Huntington: Our Sunday Visitor, 2017), 78.

Group Discussion

1. What stood out to you during your conversation?

2. Given our discussion here, what are some key elements to a good friendship?

3. What can get in the way of good friendships?

4. Have you ever considered God to be a friend? How is friendship with God similar and dissimilar to the friendships you just reflected on?

5. How would you assess your friendship with God?

Scripture & Tradition

Please invite a participant to read the following passage aloud.

Reading

No matter where you may be with God, he calls each of us into deeper communion, a closer relationship, and, yes, even an intimate friendship with him. Yet many of us find it challenging to think about God as our friend. It somehow feels too familiar, too irreverent, or even childish. We are more comfortable with a loftier God, a more cosmic Christ, a God marked more by majesty and mystery than familiarity. Reflecting upon the divinity of Christ, St. Paul wrote to the community of believers in Colossae:

Colossians 1:15-20

[15]He is the image of the invisible God, the first-born of all creation; [16]for in him all things were created, in heaven and on earth, visible and invisible, whether thrones or dominions or principalities or authorities — all things were created through him and for him. [17]He is before all things, and in him all things hold together. [18]He is the head of the body, the church; he is the beginning, the first-born from the dead, that in everything he might be pre-eminent. [19]For in him all the fulness of God was pleased to dwell, [20]and through him to reconcile to himself all things, whether on earth or in heaven, making peace by the blood of his cross.

1. How do you think about or understand God? Is God more distant for you or is he close? Familiar or removed? Personable or inaccessible? Explain.

2. What are some of the fears we all share in opening ourselves up to a friendship with Jesus?

Christ is the foundation and center of history;
he is its meaning and ultimate goal.
—Pope St. John Paul II, *Novo Millennio Ineunte*, 5

Please invite two participants to read the following selections aloud.

Reading

You might find that Paul's image of Christ in the passage from his letter to the Colossians reflects the way you feel about God. This majestic portrait of Jesus Christ is wondrous, awe inspiring, and absolutely true. Yet it would fall short of revealing the fuller nature of God if it did not also disclose the thoroughly personal, familiar, and human side of the Lord. While most of us are very comfortable with God as Creator, many of us don't know what to do with a God who calls us into intimate friendship with him.

Reading

Are we not perhaps all afraid in some way? If we let Christ enter fully into our lives, if we open ourselves totally to him, are we not afraid that he might take something away from us? Are we not perhaps afraid to give up something significant, something unique, something that makes life so beautiful? Do we not then risk ending up diminished and deprived of our freedom? And once again the pope [St. John Paul II] said: No! If we let Christ into our lives, we lose nothing, nothing, absolutely nothing of what makes life free, beautiful, and great. No! Only in this friendship are the doors of life opened wide. Only in this friendship is the great potential of human existence truly revealed. Only in this friendship do we experience beauty and liberation. And so, today, with great strength and great conviction, on the basis of long personal experience of life, I say to you, dear young people: Do not be afraid of Christ! He takes nothing away, and he gives you everything. When we give ourselves to him, we receive a hundredfold in return. Yes, open, open wide the doors to Christ—and you will find true life. Amen.[3]

1. What spoke to you in this passage?

2. What challenged you in this passage?

3. Whether now or in your past, can you identify with the fear Pope Benedict XVI describes here? Explain.

4. What does Pope Benedict XVI say will result if we open ourselves to the Lord?

5. How have you experienced some of the "beauty and liberation" of friendship with Jesus? Or in what way do you long for more of this?

Encountering Christ This Week

St. Augustine understood the human condition as restless until finding eternal peace in God, our Creator, when he wrote, "You have made us for yourself, O Lord, and our heart is restless until it rests in you."[4] To this restlessness, Jesus speaks, "Come to me, all who labor and are heavy laden, and I will give you rest" (Matthew 11:28). Take some time this week to come to Jesus with your anxieties, your weariness, and your burdens. Call out to the One who knows your need and who longs to bring you fulfillment and eternal joy in him.

---

[3] Pope Benedict XVI, Homily at the Mass for the Inauguration of the Pontificate, https://w2.vatican.va/content/benedict-xvi/en/homilies/2005/documents/hf_ben-xvi_hom_20050424_inizio-pontificato.html.

[4] Saint Augustine, *Confessions* (New York, NY: Oxford World's Classics, 1998), 3.

Look up and pray with the following "Readings for Prayerful Reflection This Week," spending time with one passage each day.

Prioritize spending some unstructured time reading, reflecting on, and praying with the passages. If you desire more structure and guidance for praying with Scripture, see appendix B. You will also be directed to appendix B in future weeks, so you need not digest it in this first week.

Readings for Prayerful Reflection This Week

- Psalm 139

- John 14:1-14

- Matthew 11:25-30

- John 8:28-32

- Isaiah 55:1-3

- Proverbs 3:5-6

Closing Reflection & Prayer

The following is a reflection by the Missionaries of Charity Fathers, written as God speaking to us. Invite a participant to read it aloud. Then take time for any spontaneous prayers of petition, praise, and thanksgiving before closing with a traditional prayer such as the Lord's Prayer.

I Thirst for You[5]

It is true. I stand at the door of your heart, day and night. Even when you are not listening, even when you doubt it could be Me, I am there. I await even the smallest sign of your response, even the least whispered invitation that will allow Me to enter.

And I want you to know that whenever you invite Me, I do come—always, without fail. Silent and unseen I come, but with infinite power and love, and bringing the many gifts of My Spirit. I come with My mercy, with My desire to forgive and heal you, and with a love for you beyond your comprehension—a love every bit as great as the love I have received from the Father. . . . I come—longing to console you and give you strength, to lift you up and bind all your wounds. . . .

Come to Me with your . . . troubles and needs, and with all your longing to be loved. . . . Open to Me, for I THIRST FOR YOU.

---

[5] Missionaries of Charity Fathers, "*I Thirst for You,*" http://www.mcfathers. org/i-thirst-for-you.html.

SESSION

Jesus:
True Source of Life

*Indeed I count everything as loss because of the surpassing
worth of knowing Christ Jesus my Lord.*
Philippians 3:8

Opening Prayer

Read the following prayer by St. John Vianney (1786–1859):

Sweet it is when we set our hearts on loving you, my
God. It sometimes happens that the more we know
our neighbors, the less we love them; but with you, O
God, it is never so. The more we know, the more we
love you.

My Jesus, how sweet it is to love you. Let me be like the
disciples on Mount Tabor, seeing nothing else but you,

my Savior. Let us be as two friends, neither of whom
can ever offend the other. Amen. [6]

Sharing Our Experience

Last week, we began discussing the topic of friendship with
Jesus. We will continue to explore this idea this week.

1. How did you experience friendship with Jesus in
    the past week?

2. Did any of the assigned Scripture passages speak
    to you?

3. Did you encounter any particular joys or challenges?

Scripture & Tradition

Reading

John 15:1-15

[1]"I am the true vine, and my Father is the vinedresser. [2]Every branch of mine that bears no fruit, he
takes away, and every branch that does bear fruit he
prunes, that it may bear more fruit. [3]You are already
made clean by the word which I have spoken to you.
[4]Abide in me, and I in you. As the branch cannot bear
fruit by itself, unless it abides in the vine, neither can
you, unless you abide in me. [5]I am the vine, you are
the branches. He who abides in me, and I in him,

---

[6] Judith A. Bauer, *The Essential Catholic Prayer Book: A Collection of
Private and Community Prayers*, (Liguori, MO: Liguori Publications, 1999),
42-43.

he it is that bears much fruit, for apart from me you can do nothing. [6] If a man does not abide in me, he is cast forth as a branch and withers; and the branches are gathered, thrown into the fire and burned. [7] If you abide in me, and my words abide in you, ask whatever you will, and it shall be done for you. [8] By this my Father is glorified, that you bear much fruit, and so prove to be my disciples. [9] As the Father has loved me, so have I loved you; abide in my love. [10] If you keep my commandments, you will abide in my love, just as I have kept my Father's commandments and abide in his love. [11] These things I have spoken to you, that my joy may be in you, and that your joy may be full.

[12] "This is my commandment, that you love one another as I have loved you. [13] Greater love has no man than this, that a man lay down his life for his friends. [14] You are my friends if you do what I command you. [15] No longer do I call you servants, for the servant does not know what his master is doing; but I have called you friends, for all that I have heard from my Father I have made known to you."

1. What are some of the recurring phrases in this passage?

2. What do you think it means to "abide in" Jesus (John 15:4)? (Some translations say "remain in.")

3. What is the relationship between the vine and the branches? How does this metaphor help us to understand what Jesus is saying to us here?

4. What are some practical ways to abide in Jesus? Also, does the passage give any guidance for this?

5. What does this passage have to teach us about our friendship with Jesus? What do you see here that connects to our discussion of friendship from last session — or deepens it?

6. In John 6:56, Jesus said, "He who eats my flesh and drinks my blood abides in me, and I in him." How does Jesus' teaching in John 6:56 complement this passage?

7. How would you explain pruning from God's (the vinedresser's/gardener's) perspective? How would you explain pruning from your perspective (a branch)?

8. What kind of pruning have you experienced in your spiritual life? Has the Lord ever helped free you from an attachment that was hindering your growth and fruitfulness? Describe what it was like to go through the pruning. What was the result?

9. Did the pruning and the results of the pruning have an impact on your friendship with Jesus?

10. Where do you currently see yourself in this passage?

Encountering Christ This Week

Reflect on the ways your life is sustained and enlivened by Jesus. How is your connection to the vine? Is there one way you could strengthen this connection this week? Write it down and make a plan to follow through.

Readings for Prayerful Reflection This Week

See appendix B for methods and guidance for praying with Scripture.

- Psalm 23

- John 10:1-18

- Romans 8:31-39

- Philippians 2:1-11

Prepare for Sunday Mass by meditating on the Scripture readings from Mass.[7]

Closing Reflection & Prayer

Invite a participant to prayerfully read the following excerpts from John 15, which are contained in the passage the group just discussed. Repetition is helpful for prayer. Then invite spontaneous prayers from the group before closing with a traditional prayer of your choice.

John 15:7-8, 12-15

> [7]If you abide in me, and my words abide in you, ask whatever you will, and it shall be done for you. [8]By this my Father is glorified, that you bear much fruit, and so prove to be my disciples. . . .

---

[7] To find the readings go to www.usccb.org/nab or download the mobile application *Laudate* and click on "Daily Readings." You can also find the complete text for the daily and Sunday Mass readings in *Abide in My Word*, published by The Word Among Us Press each year.

[12]"This is my commandment, that you love one another as I have loved you. [13]Greater love has no man than this, that a man lay down his life for his friends. [14]You are my friends if you do what I command you. [15] No longer do I call you servants, for the servant does not know what his master is doing; but I have called you friends, for all that I have heard from my Father I have made known to you.

SESSION 3

Prayer

Lord, teach us to pray.
Luke 11:1

Opening Prayer

Invite a participant to read the following prayer by St. Augustine (354–430), before concluding with a spontaneous prayer.

> 'You are great, Lord, and highly to be praised . . . : great is your power and your wisdom is immeasurable' . . . You stir man to take pleasure in praising you, because you have made us for yourself, and our heart is restless until it rests in you.[8]

Invite a participant to read the following introductory paragraph.

---

[8] Saint Augustine, *Confessions*, 3.

St. Augustine, in perhaps his most praised work, *Confessions*, remarked, "You have made us for yourself, and our heart is restless until it rests in You." In today's fast-paced world, it is not difficult to relate to such a statement. It has been said that ours is the age of restlessness. Long hours, heightened pressures, never-ending task lists, and overwhelming demands have many of us running ragged and pulled in a thousand directions. Even when we do settle in at home, social media, email, text messages, and everything else beckoning on the internet leave us as harried and distracted as we often are at work. It seems that all of our lives, no matter how hard we try to simplify, are characterized by restlessness.

Sharing Our Experience

1. What kinds of things make you restless?

2. What do you do to relieve stress in your life?

3. What prevents you from being able to be still, rest, and reflect on your life?

Invite a participant to read the following passage aloud.

Reading

Socrates once quipped, "An unexamined life is not worth living."9 Observing the nature of humanity, an Indian holy man noted, "Mind racing—madman;

---

9 Plato, *Apology* (Project Gutenberg, 2008), EBook.

mind quiet—saint; mind still—God."[10] From the divine revelation of Sacred Scripture, the psalmist puts it this way: "Be still, and know that I am God" (Psalm 46:10). To stop, to quiet ourselves, and to reflect on our lives and the One who created us are some of the first steps of knowing the all-knowing, all-present, and all-powerful reality of God. This quieting is one way that we might begin to think about a foundational aspect of the Christian life—prayer.

- How would you define prayer?

Scripture & Tradition

Please invite three participants to read the following passages.

"For me, prayer is a surge of the heart; it is a simple look turned toward heaven, it is a cry of recognition and of love, embracing both trial and joy."
—St. Thérèse of Lisieux[11]

"Contemplative rayer in my opinion is nothing else than a close sharing between friends; it means taking time frequently to be alone with him who we know loves us."
—St. Teresa of Ávila[12]

"'To pray is to talk with God. But about what?' About what? About him, and yourself: joys, sorrows, successes and failures, great ambitions, daily worries—even your weaknesses! And acts of thanksgiving and petitions—and love and reparation.

---

[10] Donald Nicholl, *Holiness* (New York: Paulist Press, 1987), 64.

[11] *Catechism*, 2558.

[12] *Catechism*, 2709.

In short, to get to know him and to get to know yourself—'to get acquainted!'"

—St. Josemaría Escrivá[13]

1. Do you relate to any of these definitions of prayer? Explain.

2. How do you pray? What are some of the ways you speak to or abide with Christ?

Reading

Luke 11:1-13

[1] He was praying in a certain place, and when he ceased, one of his disciples said to him, "Lord, teach us to pray, as John taught his disciples." [2] And he said to them, "When you pray, say:

"Father, hallowed be thy name. Thy kingdom come. [3] Give us each day our daily bread; [4] and forgive us our sins, for we ourselves forgive every one who is indebted to us; and lead us not into temptation."

[5] And he said to them, "Which of you who has a friend will go to him at midnight and say to him, 'Friend, lend me three loaves; [6] for a friend of mine has arrived on a journey, and I have nothing to set before him'; [7] and he will answer from within, 'Do not bother me; the door is now shut, and my children are with me in bed; I cannot get up and give you anything'? [8] I tell you, though he will not get up and give him anything because he is his friend, yet because of his importunity he will rise and give him whatever he needs. [9] And

---

[13] St. Josemaria Escrivá, *The Way: The Essential Classic of Opus Dei's Founder* (New York: Random House, 1982), 91.

I tell you, Ask, and it will be given you; seek, and you will find; knock, and it will be opened to you. [10]For every one who asks receives, and he who seeks finds, and to him who knocks it will be opened. [11]What father among you, if his son asks for a fish, will instead of a fish give him a serpent; [12]or if he asks for an egg, will give him a scorpion? [13]If you then, who are evil, know how to give good gifts to your children, how much more will the heavenly Father give the Holy Spirit to those who ask him!"

1. If you had to break down the parts of the Our Father into different types of prayer, how would you do so (e.g., petition, praise, thanksgiving, confession, etc.)?

2. What part is most meaningful to you? Why?

3. What type of prayer is most challenging or foreign to you?

4. When you reflect on the way you pray, are there other aspects of prayer contained in the Lord's Prayer that might broaden your prayer?

5. What analogy does this passage give to help us realize the perfect heavenly Father that we pray to?

6. Has parenting or mentoring children helped you better understand God's heart for his children (us)? If so, how? How might that apply to conversing with God, petitioning God, and receiving from God?

7. How do you understand Jesus' promises to those who ask, seek and knock? What is your reaction to this part of the passage?

Encountering Christ This Week

Is it better to pray by reading a formal prayer of the Church, perhaps drawn from the rich history of our tradition? Or is it more pleasing to God that we pray with our own words or, as many have put it, that we "pray from the heart"? Of course, both methods are encouraged by the Church as wonderful ways to express our faith, hope, and love of God. Some Christians, however, may only be comfortable with reciting a prayer written by another, typically a noted saint or icon of the faith. Spontaneous prayer may seem too personal, vulnerable, or even intimidating. Though both types of prayer are good, necessary, and encouraged by the Church, there is a benefit for a renewed emphasis on praying spontaneously, using not only another's words but your own.

Peter Kreeft, noted author and professor of philosophy at Boston College, commented,

> When we use the prayers of the Church, we use the greatest prayers ever written, the words and sentiments of great saints and hymn writers and liturgists. We do this rightly, because God deserves the best, and these prayers are the best. They were composed by other people, but we make them our own when we pray them, like a lover reciting a sonnet by Shakespeare to his beloved. . . .

> But if others' words are the *only* words lovers use to each other, they are not lovers but performers. We must not only "say our prayers," we must *pray*. Others' words may be more beautiful, but your words are more yours, and God cherishes them as a father cherishes his child's own crude drawing made just for him more than he cherishes the greatest work of art in the world.

God wants your own words most of all because they are your own; they come from your heart, and your heart is what your Lover craves."[14]

This week, try devoting at least 10 to 15 minutes a day to spending some time alone with the Lord. Pray from the heart. There is no wrong way to talk to God. Talk about anything on your mind. Keep it real; don't just say what you think a prayerful person should say or what you think God wants to hear. Even saying, "Lord, help me to pray" is itself a prayer.

Keep in mind three of the first things we all learn to say as children: "Thank you," "I'm sorry," and "Please." That's a great outline for a chat with God! Also, take a little time to listen "with the ear of your heart" to God's voice deep within you, or just rest in silence and stillness, aware of God's presence (*Rule of St. Benedict*, Prologue, 1).

See appendix C for another helpful outline for praying from the heart.

Closing Reflection & Prayer

Invite a participant to read the following prayer. Afterwards, invite participants to add their own prayers. Close the group at the appropriate time.

Almighty God and Father,

Over this last week, I have tried to understand your love for me and the entire people of God you created for your glory. I don't claim to fully understand your love, but I am trying to open myself to you and the love you have planned for me from the beginning.

I know that you have loved me and blessed me in ways I could not have imagined.

---

[14] Peter Kreeft, *Prayer for Beginners*, (San Francisco: Ignatius Press), 29-30

So please, dear Father, help me to remember your great love—when I wonder about my worthiness, when I fall into doubt, when I am inclined to be unloving.

I want your love to be reflected in my daily life. Thank you for loving us in a way we can understand. And thank you for loving us first. Amen.

SESSION 4

A Habit of Prayer

My secret is simple. I pray.
—St. Teresa of Calcutta[15]

Opening Prayer

Invite a participant to read the following prayer from the Catholic Tradition. Conclude with a spontaneous prayer.

> Lord, I believe in you; increase my faith.
> I trust in you; strengthen my trust.
> I love you: let me love you more and more.
> I am sorry for my sins: deepen my sorrow
>
> I worship you as my first beginning,
> I long for you as my last end,
> I praise you as my constant helper,
> And call on you as my loving protector.
> Amen.[16]

---

[15] Dale Salwak, ed., *The Power of Prayer* (Novato, CA: New World Library, 1998), 3.

[16] From *"The Universal Prayer"* as cited in Judith A. Bauer, 45-46.

Sharing Our Experience

Last week, we began discussing the mysterious and beautiful call to prayer. We will continue to explore this idea this week.

1. How did you pray in the past week?

2. Were you able to devote 10 to 15 minutes a day in conversational prayer, as encouraged in last session's "Encountering Christ This Week" section?

3. Did you encounter any specific joys or challenges?

Scripture & Tradition

Reading

Philippians 4:4-9

[4] Rejoice in the Lord always; again I will say, Rejoice. [5] Let all men know your forbearance. The Lord is at hand. [6] Have no anxiety about anything, but in everything by prayer and supplication with thanksgiving let your requests be made known to God. [7] And the peace of God, which passes all understanding, will keep your hearts and your minds in Christ Jesus. [8] Finally, brethren, whatever is true, whatever is honorable, whatever is just, whatever is pure, whatever is lovely, whatever is gracious, if there is any excellence, if there is anything worthy of praise, think about these things. [9] What you have learned and received and heard and seen in me, do; and the God of peace will be with you.

1. What promise is contained in this passage?

2. Some translations use the word "guard" instead of "keep" in verse 7. How does this word change or deepen your understanding of what St. Paul is saying here?

3. What concrete advice does St. Paul give, which can lead us deeper into the peace "which passes all understanding"?

4. What are some practical ways you practice St. Paul's advice in daily life?

5. How have you recently experienced peace beyond understanding as a result of Jesus? Or in what way do you need peace right now in your life?

6. What else strikes you about this passage, and why?

Reading

"The Our Father begins with a great consolation: we are allowed to say 'Father.' This one word contains the whole history of redemption. We are allowed to say 'Father,' because the Son was our brother and has revealed the Father to us; because, thanks to what Christ has done, we have once more become children of God." . . .

We must therefore let Jesus teach us what *father* really means. . . . The love that endures "to the end" (John 13:1), which the Lord fulfilled on the Cross in praying for his enemies, shows us the essence of the Father. . . .

Let us consider a further text as well. The Lord reminds us that fathers do not give their children stones when they ask for bread. He then goes on to say: "If you then, who are evil, know how to give good gifts to your children, how much more will your Father who is in heaven give good things to those who ask him!" (Matthew 7:9). Luke specifies the "good gifts" that the Father gives; he says "how much more will the heavenly Father give the Holy Spirit to those who ask him!" (Luke 11:13). This means that the gift of God is God himself. The "good things" that he gives us are himself. This reveals in a surprising way what prayer is really all about: It is not about this or that, but about God's desire to offer us the gift of himself—that is the gift of all gifts, the "one thing necessary." Prayer is a way of gradually purifying and correcting our wishes and of slowly coming to realize what we really need: God and his Spirit.[17]

1. What spoke to you from this passage?

2. According to Pope Benedict, what is the gift of God?

3. How does this view of what happens in prayer and what we receive in prayer affect your understanding of prayer?

4. Where and when do you pray? What is your style of prayer? Do you speak aloud or sit quietly? What has worked for you?

5. What are some practical measures that have helped you to regularly set aside time for prayer?

---

[17] Pope Benedict, *Jesus of Nazareth* (New York: Doubleday, 2007), 135-137.

Encountering Christ This Week

*Morning by morning he wakens,
he wakens my ear to hear.*
Isaiah 50:4

It is crucial to find time in your life to pray every day. Identify a time when you can get up and find a solitary place to pray. Make prayer a first priority in your day. Open your ears that you may truly hear God's eternal Word, Jesus Christ our Lord. Commit to a certain duration for prayer, and guard it in your schedule as you would guard a date with a special friend.

If you have not yet read the list of "Tips for Building a Daily Habit of Prayer" in appendix B, make sure to do so this week before proceeding to the "Readings for Prayerful Reflection This Week" below.

If possible, try to also attend daily Mass and/or go to the Sacrament of Reconciliation this week. At Mass, Jesus makes clear his desire for friendship and connection with us through the Scripture readings and by giving his life to us in the Eucharist. Confession gives us a chance to heal our friendship with Christ if we know that we have done things to hinder it. (See appendix D: "A Guide to the Sacrament of Reconciliation.")

Readings for Prayerful Reflection This Week

See appendix B for methods and guidance for praying with Scripture.

- Luke 12:22-32

- Matthew 6:1-8

- Jeremiah 29:12-14

- Ephesians 3:14-21

- Psalm 27

Closing Reflection & Prayer

Invite a participant to read aloud the following prayer inspired by St. Cyprian of Carthage (ca. 200–258). Then invite each participant to offer their own spontaneous prayers.

We pray to you, Lord, with honest hearts, in tune with one another, entreating you with sighs and tears, as befits our humble position—placed, as we are, between the spiritually weak who have no concern for you and the saints who stand firm and upright before you. We pray that you may soon come to us, leading us from darkness to light, oppression to freedom, misery to joy, conflict to peace. May you drive away the storms and tempests of our lives, and bring gentle calm. We pray that you will care for us, as a father cares for his children. Amen.[18]

---

[18] Jacquelyn Lindsey, ed., *Catholic Prayers for All Occasions* (Huntington, Indiana: Our Sunday Visitor, 2017), 49.

SESSION

Sacred Scripture

For the word of God is living and active.
Hebrews 4:12

Opening Prayer

Invite a participant to pray the following prayer attributed to Origen (ca. 185–254).

Prayer for Knowledge of Scripture

Lord, inspire us to read your Scriptures and to meditate upon them day and night. We beg you to give us real understanding of what we need, that we in turn may put its precepts into practice. Yet we know that understanding and good intentions are worthless, unless rooted in your graceful love. So we ask that the words of Scriptures may also be not just signs on a page, but channels of grace into our hearts.[19]

We pray this through Jesus Christ, our Lord. Amen.

---

[19] Adapted into plural from https://www.catholicity.com/prayer/prayer-for-knowledge-of-scripture.html

Sharing Our Experience

In the last session, we discussed how prayer is a wellspring of grace, a central and essential means to communion or friendship with Jesus. Today's reflection on Sacred Scripture is related to personal prayer. As the Dogmatic Constitution on Divine Revelation (*Dei Verbum*), 25 from Vatican II states,

> . . . [P]rayer should accompany the reading of Sacred Scripture, so that God and man may talk together; for "we speak to Him when we pray; we hear Him when we read the divine saying."[20]

Each one of us comes to this group with different conceptions of and experiences with Scripture.

1. What comes to mind when you hear the word "Bible"?

2. What has been your experience of Scripture?

Scripture & Tradition

Invite a participant to read the following passage aloud.

Reading

Hebrews 4:12-13

[12] For the word of God is living and active, sharper than any two-edged sword, piercing to the division of soul and spirit, of joints and marrow, and discerning the thoughts and intentions of the heart. [13] And before him no creature is hidden, but all are open and laid bare to the eyes of him with whom we have to do.

---

[20] *Dei Verbum*, 25.

1. What does the metaphor "sharper than any two-edged sword, piercing . . . soul and spirit, of joints and marrow" mean to you? What do you think the writer of Hebrews wants us to understand by this image? (Take a few moments to go back over the passage and to reflect before sharing.)

2. Can you explain in practical terms how the word of God discerns "the thoughts and intentions of the heart" (Hebrews 4:12)?

3. Have you ever experienced the word of God becoming "living" to you, touching your heart and mind in a way that changed you—in a big or small way?

Reading

Document from the Second Vatican Council, *Dei Verbum*:

The Church has always venerated the divine Scriptures just as she venerates the body of the Lord, since, especially in the sacred liturgy, she unceasingly receives and offers to the faithful the bread of life from the table both of God's word and of Christ's body. She has always maintained them, and continues to do so, together with Sacred Tradition, as the supreme rule of faith, since, as inspired by God and committed once and for all to writing, they impart the word of God Himself without change, and make the voice of the Holy Spirit resound in the words of the prophets and Apostles. Therefore, like the Christian religion itself, all the preaching of the Church must be nourished and regulated by Sacred Scripture. For in the sacred books, the Father who is in heaven meets His children with great love and speaks with them; and the force and power in the word of God is so great that it stands as the support and energy of the Church, the strength of faith for her sons, the food of the soul, the pure and everlasting source of spiritual life. Consequently these words are perfectly applicable to Sacred Scripture: "For the word of God is living and active" (Hebrews 4:12) and "it has power to build you up and give you your heritage among all those who are sanctified" (Acts 20:32; see 1 Thessalonians 2:13).[21]

1. What are some of the statements that describe how highly the Church regards Sacred Scripture?

2. How does the Church describe the impact that Scripture can have on one's relationship to Christ?

3. Catholics are known for how highly they esteem and venerate (honor, reverence) the Body of the Lord (the Eucharist.) What do you think it means that "[t]he Church has always venerated the divine Scriptures just as she venerates the body of the Lord"?

4. What is meant by "Sacred Tradition"? How do Sacred Scripture and Sacred Tradition work together to lead us in understanding what God has revealed?

5. How do you explain that the Father "meets His children with great love and speaks with them" when they read Scripture?

[21] Pope Paul VI, *Dei Verbum*, November 18, 1965, 25, http://www.vatican.va/archive/hist_councils/ii_vatican_council/documents/vat-ii_const_19651118_dei-verbum_en.html..

6. Do these words from Sacred Tradition add any-
    thing to your understanding of the previous discus-
    sion about the Hebrews 4 passage?

7. What from this passage challenges or inspires
    you? How?

*It must be said that Sacred Scripture is divinely ordered
to this: that through it, the truth necessary for salvation
may be made known to us.*
—St. Thomas Aquinas[22]

Encountering Christ This Week

Read or review appendix B, "A Guide to Seeking God in Prayer
and Scripture," before moving on to the suggested readings for
prayerful reflection below. Utilize the "4 R" method of *lectio divina* to help you converse with God through the following Scripture passages. Pray with only one Scripture reading per day.

Readings for Prayerful Reflection
This Week

- Psalm 19

- 2 Timothy 3:10-17

- Deuteronomy 30:10-14

- Joshua 1:1-9

---

[22] Raimondo Spiazzi, ed., *Quaestiones Quodlibetales* (Turin: Marietti,
    1956), 146.

Prepare for Sunday Mass by meditating on the Scripture readings from Mass.

Closing Reflection & Prayer

After someone opens the group in prayer, take time for spontaneous prayers of petition, thanksgiving, and praise. Then pray the following psalm. Invite a few readers or go around the circle, each reading a paragraph.

Psalm 119:89-105

89   For ever, O Lord, thy word
    is firmly fixed in the heavens.
90   Thy faithfulness endures to all generations;
    thou hast established the earth, and it stands
    fast.
91   By thy appointment they stand this day;
    for all things are thy servants.
92   If thy law had not been my delight,
    I should have perished in my affliction.
93   I will never forget thy precepts;
    for by them thou hast given me life.
94   I am thine, save me;
    for I have sought thy precepts.
95   The wicked lie in wait to destroy me;
    but I consider thy testimonies.
96   I have seen a limit to all perfection,
    but thy commandment is exceedingly broad.
97   Oh, how I love thy law!
    It is my meditation all the day.
98   Thy commandment makes me wiser than
    my enemies,
    for it is ever with me.

99 I have more understanding than all my teachers,
for thy testimonies are my meditation.
100 I understand more than the aged,
for I keep thy precepts.
101 I hold back my feet from every evil way,
in order to keep thy word.
102 I do not turn aside from thy ordinances,
for thou hast taught me.
103 How sweet are thy words to my taste,
sweeter than honey to my mouth!
104 Through thy precepts I get understanding;
therefore I hate every false way.
105 Thy word is a lamp to my feet
and a light to my path.

We pray this through Jesus Christ, our Lord. Amen.

Reactions to the Word of God

The Word of God is in your heart. The Word digs in this soil so that the spring may gush out.
—Origen (ca. 185–254)[23]

Opening Prayer

Invite a participant to read the following excerpt from Psalm 19:7-10. Then conclude with a spontaneous prayer.

7   The law of the LORD is perfect,
        reviving the soul;
    the testimony of the LORD is sure,
        making wise the simple;
8   the precepts of the LORD are right,
        rejoicing the heart;
    the commandment of the LORD is pure,

---

[23] Thomas C. Oden, *Life in the Spirit* (San Francisco: Harper Collins, 1992), 293.

enlightening the eyes;
9   the fear of the LORD is clean,
enduring for ever;
the ordinances of the LORD are true,
and righteous altogether.
10   More to be desired are they than gold,
even much fine gold;
sweeter also than honey
and drippings of the honeycomb.

Sharing Our Experience

Last week, we discussed the role that Sacred Scripture plays in our friendship with Christ. This week we will continue to explore this theme.

1. How did you pray with Scripture during the past week?

2. Did any of the assigned Scripture passages speak to you?

3. Did you encounter any particular joys or challenges?

Scripture & Tradition

The following reading explores different reactions that people have to the word of God. Invite two participants to read the following sections aloud.

Mark 4:1-9, 13-20

[1]Again he began to teach beside the sea. And a very large crowd gathered about him, so that he got into a boat and sat in it on the sea; and the whole crowd was beside the sea on the land. [2]And he taught them many things in parables, and in his teaching he said to them: [3]"Listen! A sower went out to sow. [4]And as he sowed, some seed fell along the path, and the birds came and devoured it. [5]Other seed fell on rocky ground, where it had not much soil, and immediately it sprang up, since it had no depth of soil; [6]and when the sun rose it was scorched, and since it had no root it withered away. [7]Other seed fell among thorns and the thorns grew up and choked it, and it yielded no grain. [8]And other seeds fell into good soil and brought forth grain, growing up and increasing and yielding thirtyfold and sixtyfold and a hundredfold." [9]And he said, "He who has ears to hear, let him hear."

. . .

[13]And he said to them, "Do you not understand this parable? How then will you understand all the parables? [14]The sower sows the word. [15]And these are the ones along the path, where the word is sown; when they hear, Satan immediately comes and takes away the word which is sown in them. [16]And these in like manner are the ones sown upon rocky ground, who, when they hear the word, immediately receive it with joy; [17]and they have no root in themselves, but endure for a while; then, when tribulation or persecution arises on account of the word, immediately they fall away. [18]And others are the ones sown among

thorns; they are those who hear the word, [19]but the cares of the world, and the delight in riches, and the desire for other things, enter in and choke the word, and it proves unfruitful. [20]But those that were sown upon the good soil are the ones who hear the word and accept it and bear fruit, thirtyfold and sixtyfold and a hundredfold."

1. What does Jesus say the seed represents (see verses 4 and 14)?

2. Describe the different human responses to the word of God that each type of soil represents.

3. Jesus likens "rocky ground" to the person who has no root in themselves. They receive the word with joy and endure for a while, but when tribulation comes "on account of the word," they fall away. What are some contemporary tribulations that could come "on account of the word"?

4. What might be some modern-day thorns? And how can they choke out the word of God in a person's heart?

5. What else strikes you or piques your interest from this parable?

6. Take a couple of minutes in silence to reflect on and even write down which type(s) of soil you most identify with and why. Then come together as a group and share.

Please invite a participant to read the following section aloud.

In all relationships, communication is essential to growth and intimacy. Our relationship with Christ is no different. The more we listen to God as we read Scripture, the more we get to know Jesus Christ and hear the Holy Spirit speak to us personally in our daily lives. St. Jerome went so far as to say that "ignorance of the Scriptures is ignorance of Christ."[24] In addition, the Church "earnestly and especially urges all the Christian faithful . . . to learn . . . 'the excellent knowledge of Jesus Christ' (Philippians 3:8) by frequent reading of the divine Scriptures."[25] The Church also teaches that "prayer should accompany the reading of Sacred Scripture, so that God and man may talk together; for "we speak to Him when we pray; we hear Him when we read the divine saying."[26]

1.   What stands out to you from this passage?

2.   What are some practical ways to integrate Scripture into daily life and prayer?

Encountering Christ This Week

Set aside a place and time each day when you can read Scripture, reflect, and pray. Once again, see appendices B and C if you need help.

Reflect on your current experiences of prayer:

1.   How is the habit of prayer going for you?

---

[24] *Catechism*, 133.

[25] *Dei Verbum*, 25.

[26] *Dei Verbum*, 25.

2. What joys and challenges are you facing?

3. To what extent are *lectio divina* and Scripture helping you tune into the Lord's voice?

4. What questions do you have about prayer or Scripture that you might ask a friend, pastor or mentor about?

Readings for Prayerful Reflection This Week

- Matthew 5:13-20

- Mark 10:17-31

- 2 Corinthians 4:16–5:10

In preparation for Sunday's liturgy, or as a daily practice, read and pray with the Mass readings.

> *All Sacred Scripture is but one book,*
> *and that one book is Christ.*[27]
> —Hugh of St. Victor (ca. 1096–1141)

Closing Reflection & Prayer

Invite participants to pray spontaneously about the themes of today's session and anything else on their hearts. Close with the following traditional prayer from the Catholic tradition, which can be used in personal prayer after a time of prayer and/or Scripture meditation.

---

[27] *Catechism*, 134.

Prayer After Meditation[28]

I thank you, my God, for the good resolutions, affections and inspirations that you have communicated to me in this meditation. I beg your help in putting them into effect. My Immaculate Mother, Saint Joseph my father and lord, my guardian angel, intercede for me.

---

[28] CatholiCity, *Prayer After Meditation*, https://www.catholicity.com/prayer/prayer-after-meditation.html.

Conclusions on These Sessions of *The Way*

As mentioned in the introduction to these sessions, *The Way* seeks to be more than a Bible study. Our hope and purpose are to encourage an authentic encounter with Jesus Christ, the source and summit of our faith. As they were for the disciples so long ago on the road to Emmaus, we hope that your hearts were burning as you encountered Jesus personally through word and sacrament, reflection and discussion, solitude and community.

For some, the last several weeks may have spurred a spiritual awakening of sorts. Your faith in Jesus Christ and your friendship with him may have deepened, strengthened, and taken on a richer, fuller context. Perhaps this was the first time you have ever opened yourself to a deeply personal friendship with Jesus Christ. Maybe this small group has helped you to overcome misconceptions or even fears about the spiritual life. Or perhaps you already knew and practiced much of what was discussed in these sessions, but now you are renewed in your journey and surrounded by a stronger community.

Regardless of your experience through *The Way*, the journey is not over. First off, there's another volume! Don't miss out on the explorations of the topics of ongoing conversion, Eucharist, community, and mission in *The Way, Part 2*! What's more, Jesus continues to walk alongside us every day, meeting us where we are yet calling us to a place we have not yet been. Not only as master but as a friend, Jesus calls us to "put out into the deep" (*Novo Millenio Ineunte*, 1), to embrace the mystery of a life spent knowing, loving, and serving him.

Just as in human friendships, our ongoing friendship with God requires time, attention, and prayerful reflection. We must continue to invest in the precious gift of faith we have been given in Jesus Christ. Through *The Way* and perhaps even with the support of a small group, we hope that you continue to grow in the fundamental habits of discipleship—daily prayer, Scripture reading, embracing the rich sacramental life, authentic Christian community, openness to ongoing conversion, and living a life on mission for the gospel.

> *"Put out into the deep" . . . "Duc in altum!"*
> —St. John Paul II, *Novo Millennio Ineunte*, 1

It is vital that we continue in the practice of these disciplines in order to grow more and more into the likeness of Jesus Christ our Lord. May the conclusion of this first part of *The Way* propel you into a new springtime of growth through your ongoing commitment to faithfulness.

- Make a personal commitment to spend time alone in prayer every day. Just as Jesus so often did, break away from the noise and the busyness of daily life to find that solitary place to commune with the Father.

- Dedicate a portion of your devotional time to reading Scripture. You may wish to follow the daily readings offered by the Church (see www.usccb.org/nab/). You may also want to prayerfully discern a book or section of the Bible that you feel God calling you to read—maybe a Gospel, the psalms, or the Pauline epistles. Regardless of your particular reading selection, many find it helpful to begin with Scripture, providing spiritual "fodder" for their time in prayer.

- Commit to continuing, finding, or perhaps even starting a small Christian community in which you can continue to grow with other faithful disciples of

Christ. This can be a very beneficial aspect of your ongoing spiritual development. Meet regularly for prayer, Scripture reflection, and discussion.

- And most important, embrace Jesus in the greatest gifts he has given us: his very self in the sacraments. In addition to Sunday liturgies, make time to attend daily Mass when possible—prayerfully receiving our Lord in the Eucharist. Foster a deeper friendship with Jesus by spending time with him through Adoration of the Blessed Sacrament in your parish. Receive his forgiveness, healing, and transforming strength through the Sacrament of Reconciliation.

You have received "good news" indeed! Jesus is not in the tomb but is alive and well among us. Awakened by the presence of Emmanuel (God with us), we too are compelled to share our experience of the risen Lord with those we know and love—"The Lord has risen indeed" (Luke 24:34). May your mouth speak out of the abundance of your heart, remade and set ablaze by the power of God. And may the world come to know him through your enduring connection to Jesus Christ.

No demand on our ministry is more urgent than the
"new evangelization" needed to satisfy
the spiritual hunger of our times.[29]
—St. John Paul II

---

[29] St. John Paul II, Address of the Holy Father Pope John Paul II to the Bishops of the Episcopal Conference of the Unites States of America (New England and the Ecclesiastical Provinces of Boston and Hartford), October 24, 1998, 3, https://w2.vatican.va/content/john-paul-ii/en/speeches/1998/october/documents/hf_jp-ii_spe_19981024_ad-limina-usa.html.

APPENDICES

For Participants

A. Small Group Discussion Guide

B. A Guide to Seeking God in Prayer and Scripture

C. ACTS: A Way to Pray Every Day

D. A Guide to the Sacrament of Reconciliation

Appendix A
Small Group Discussion Guide

A small group seeks to foster an honest exploration of Jesus Christ with others. For many, this will be a new experience. You may be wondering what will take place. Will I fit in? Will I even want to come back?

Here are some expectations and values to help participants understand how small groups work, as well as what makes them work and what doesn't. When a group meets for the first time, the facilitator may want to read the following aloud and discuss it to be sure people understand small group parameters.

Purpose

We gather as searchers. Our express purpose for being here is to explore together what it means to live the gospel of Jesus Christ in and through the Church.

Priority

In order to reap the full fruit of this personal and communal journey, each one of us will make participation in the weekly gatherings a priority.

Participation

We will strive to create an environment in which all are encouraged to share at their comfort level.

We will begin and end all sessions in prayer, exploring over time ways to pray together. We will discuss a Scripture passage at every meeting. Participants do not need to read the passage beforehand—no one needs to know anything about the Bible in order to participate. The point is to discuss the text and see how it applies to our own lives.

Discussion Guidelines

The purpose of our gathering time is to share in Spirit-filled discussion. This type of dialogue occurs when the presence of the Holy Spirit is welcomed and encouraged by the nature and tenor of the discussion. To help this happen, we will observe the following guidelines:

- Participants strive always to be respectful, humble, open, and honest in listening and sharing: they don't interrupt, respond abruptly, condemn what another says, or even judge in their hearts.

- Participants share at the level that is comfortable for them personally.

- Silence is a vital part of the experience. Participants are given time to reflect before discussion begins. Keep in mind that a period of comfortable silence often occurs between individuals speaking.

- Participants are enthusiastically encouraged to share while at the same time exercising care to permit others (especially the quieter members) an opportunity to speak. Each participant should aim to maintain a balance: participating without dominating the conversation.

- Participants keep confidential anything personal that may be shared in the group.

Perhaps most important, participants should cultivate attentiveness to the Holy Spirit's desire to be present in the time spent together. When the conversation seems to need help, ask for the Holy Spirit's intercession silently in your heart. When someone is speaking of something painful or difficult, pray that the Holy Spirit comforts that person. Pray for the Spirit to aid the group in responding sensitively and lovingly. If someone isn't participating, praying for that person during silence may be more helpful than a direct question. These are but a few examples of the ways in which each person might personally invoke the Holy Spirit.

Time

We meet weekly because that is the best way to become comfortable together, but we can schedule our meetings around any breaks or holidays when many people will be away.

It is important that our group start and end on time. Generally a group meets for about ninety minutes, with an additional thirty minutes or so afterward for refreshments. Agree on these times as a group and work to honor them.

Appendix B
A Guide to Seeking God
in Prayer and Scripture

*Unless you are convinced that prayer is the best use
of your time, you will never find time to pray.*
—Fr. Hilary Ottensmeyer, OSB[30]

If only I had the time!

Time—we only have so much of it each day. All kinds of demands chip away the hours. Modern communication and social media increase our sense of urgency. No wonder we experience conflicting desires over how to spend our time.

One thing we all know for certain: relationships require time. Friendships don't form or last unless people spend time together. Marriages struggle when spouses don't make time to talk and listen deeply to one another. Parents who do not prioritize spending time with their children risk painfully regretting that decision down the road. Some things never change. We were made for relationships, and relationships take time.

So how about our relationship with God?

Just as all relationships require time, so too does a deepening friendship with God. What kind of relationship do you have with the person in your neighborhood with whom you've never had a personal conversation? Even if you take out her garbage can weekly because she is disabled, she is an acquaintance, not a friend. Friends spend time together. Jesus called us his friends (John 15:15).

---

[30] Accessed March 1, 2017, at http://www.saintmeinrad.edu/seminary-blog/
echoes-from-the-bell-tower/posts/2015/monastic-time.

One way we spend time with Jesus is at Mass. This will always be the center, source, and summit of our prayer lives. But without personal time with Jesus outside liturgies, the encounter at Mass can resemble meeting that neighbor at a block party: talking for a few minutes without any deep connection. The mysterious reality of that person remains remote.

How much time should I spend in personal prayer?

A little goes a long way with God. Start small and work up to more. If you're not already in the practice of prioritizing a prayer time daily, start with fifteen minutes if you can. If that proves too difficult, try ten or even five minutes.

Prayer begets prayer. As you experience the fruit of a deeper friendship with the Lord, your desire for God grows. Your heart longs more and more to build your life around prayer rather than just squeezing it in. Hunger for God grows when you taste the sweetness of Jesus' company and experience the joy of a Christ-centered life.

Basics of Spending Time with God in Prayer

Always begin by recognizing that God is with you. He is with you even when you're not paying attention. When you attend to God, you are simply focusing on reality.

St. Teresa of Ávila called prayer "an intimate sharing between friends."[31] Any good friendship involves three things: talking, listening, and simply being together.

---

[31] Teresa of Avila, *The Book of Her Life, translated, with notes*, by Kieran Kavanaugh, OCD, and Otilio Rodriguez, OCD (Indianapolis/Cambridge: Hackett Publishing Company, 2008), 44.

1. Talk to God

There is no wrong way to talk to God. Talk about anything on your mind. Keep it real; don't just say what you think a prayerful person should say or what you think God wants to hear. Even saying, "Lord, help me to pray" is itself a prayer.

If you're stuck, keep in mind the first three things we all learn to say as children: "Thank you," "I'm sorry," and "Please." That's a great outline for a chat with God—it's as simple as that! See also appendix C—Acts: A Way to Pray Every Day.

2. Listen to God

Morning after morning he wakens my ear to hear.

(Isaiah 50:4)

No matter how impossible it may seem, you can learn to discern the Lord's voice in your life. It takes practice and guidance, but never forget the promise of Jesus: "My sheep hear my voice, and I know them, and they follow me" (John 10:27). Jesus means what he says—this is attainable!

The fastest way to learn to recognize the voice of God is to read the Scriptures prayerfully. The Bible truly is God's word expressed in human words. With the Holy Spirit coming to our aid, reading it becomes "a life-giving encounter" (*Novo Millennio Ineunte*, 39). On the following pages, a simple outline of *lectio divina* will help you to find out what the Lord wants to say to you through Scripture. *Lectio divina* is a time-tested way of encountering the voice of the living God in Scripture.

3. Be with God

Sometimes words get in the way of deeper communication. St. John of the Cross said, "The Father spoke one Word, which was his Son, and this Word he speaks always in eternal silence, and in silence must it be heard by the soul."[32] The Lord says, "Be still, and know that I am God" (Psalm 46:10).

Begin and end each prayer time with a minute or two of silence to rest in God's presence. You probably won't hear anything audible or even sense anything interiorly, but be confident that God is filling that silence in ways you cannot immediately perceive. Often something can become very clear later in the day after a time of silence in the morning.

Lectio Divina: Putting It All Together

One of the best ways to "talk," "listen," and "be with" God in a single sitting is the time-honored method of praying with Scripture called *lectio divina* (Latin for "divine reading"). This ancient practice has seen dramatic growth in popularity since Vatican II, partly due to the loud and clear call of every pope since the council for laity and clergy alike to discover (or rediscover) this treasure. For example, Pope Benedict XVI said the following:

> I would like in particular to recall and recommend the ancient tradition of *Lectio divina:* the diligent reading of Sacred Scripture accompanied by prayer brings about that intimate dialogue in which the person reading hears God who is speaking, and in praying, responds to him with trusting openness of heart (cf. *Dei Verbum,* 25). If it is effectively promoted, this practice will bring

---

[32] *The Collected Works of St. John of the Cross*, translated by Kieran Kavanaugh, OCD, and Otilio Rodriguez, OCD (Washington, DC: ICS Publications, 1991), 92.

to the Church—I am convinced of it—a new spiritual springtime.

—Pope Benedict XVI[33]

The term *lectio divina* is often associated with St. Benedict of Nursia of the sixth century. The Rule of St. Benedict assigned monks to meditate upon Scripture at specific hours of the day. In the Middle Ages, four steps came to specify the process: *Lectio* (reading), *Meditatio* (meditation/reflection), *Oratio* (prayer) and *Contemplatio* (contemplation or resting in God's presence).

Lectio teaches us to listen intently for a specific word or phrase that stands out, whether boldly or ever so gently. As believers, we trust that the Holy Spirit aids our reading of the Scripture. When something stands out or troubles us in a reading, this is God's personal word for us to think about (meditation) and discuss with Jesus (prayer, or *oratio*).

If you find it difficult to remember the four aspects of *Lectio,* four "Rs" give a simple and memorable description: read, reflect, respond, rest. See more below.

The Four Rs: A Method for Lectio Divina

Preparation

> Begin with the Sign of the Cross.
> Take a moment to be quiet and still.
> Ask the Holy Spirit to guide your time.

---

[33] Pope Benedict XVI, Address to Participants in the International Congress Organized to Commemorate the 40th Anniversary of *Dei Verbum*, September 16, 2005, www.vatican.va, https://w2.vatican.va/content/bene- dict-xvi/en/speeches/2005/september/documents/hf_ben-xvi_spe_20050916_40-dei- verbum.html.

1. **Read** the Scripture selection slowly and attentively. Note any word, phrase, or image that catches your attention. It's helpful to read the passage more than once and/or out loud.

2. **Reflect.** Think about the meaning of whatever caught your attention. The Holy Spirit drew you to it for a reason. What line of thought do you pursue in response? Notice any questions that arise or any emotions you experience. Return to the text as often as you wish.

3. **Respond.** Talk to God about the passage, your thoughts, or anything else on your heart. Thank him for the blessings you have received. Ask him for your own needs, as well as the needs of others. Note any changes or actions you want to make. If the Holy Spirit leads you to any resolution or application in your life, writing it down will help you remember. Ask God to help you live it out.

4. **Rest.** Rest a few minutes in silence with the Lord. "Be still, and know that I am God" (Psalm 46:10). This period of rest allows the meditations and prayers of the day to sink down from your mind to your heart, as you linger in the Father's loving embrace.

Tips for Building A Daily Habit of Prayer

Schedule time

- Aim to spend some time with God in at least one uninterrupted period, not while driving or doing other activities. Don't multitask! Recall how you feel when you're in the middle of a conversation with a friend who suddenly brings out a smart phone and begins texting. It's a good habit to keep God's presence throughout the day when you're doing other things, but also dedicate a specific time to focus solely on God.

- A scheduled time helps build the habit of prayer. Setting a regular time each day is the surest way to make your prayer time happen.

- Pray in the morning if possible.

- Praying and listening to God first thing in the morning is best for many people because nothing interferes with your prayer if nothing else is happening.

- Morning prayer allows you to quite literally "seek first his kingdom" (Matthew 6:33). It also allows you the chance to make up your prayer at some later time in the day if an unforeseen circumstance interrupts your morning prayer time.

- Praying first thing in the morning has been the preferred practice of many saints and Christians throughout history, and Jesus himself often rose before dawn to pray in solitude.

- But pray how and when you can! It's more important to schedule a time each day than to schedule an ideal time you won't keep. If you cannot do your daily prayer time in the morning, we still recommend starting your day with a simple morning offering.

Don't let the "method" get in the way

The four steps of *lectio divina* can help, but don't let them limit you. Teresa of Ávila called prayer "an intimate sharing between friends." A conversation between friends would be strange and forced if it always followed a routine or formula. Try different ways to talk, listen to, and simply be with God.

Explore other prompts or methods for prayer. For example, use the Our Father or the Order of the Mass as an outline of the various types of prayer and petition.

Sometimes words get in the way of deeper communication. Lovers stare into one another's eyes wordlessly. Parents and children cuddle and say nothing. The only way to hear anyone, including God, is to be silent. Any friendship in which you are never quiet and attentive will eventually dissolve. Begin and end each prayer time with a minute of silence to rest in God's presence.

Additional Tips

- Be yourself and come to God just as you are, not how you think you should be.

- Set achievable goals.

- Don't overlook the human mechanisms that will enable you to be faithful to daily prayer: Put it on your calendar; set the coffee maker the night before so that it's ready for your morning coffee date with Jesus; make a commitment to ignore social media and email until you've prayed. Put your alarm on the other side of the room, so that you don't waste 15 minutes hitting the snooze bar!

- If you are distracted, simply persevere. Take those distractions to prayer or write them down so you can return to them at a better time. Ask your guardian angel to take care of it. God does not mind distractions. It is the love with which we return our focus to him that he desires. Many find it helpful to use a small notebook or journal to help focus their payer times.

- Do not overidealize your prayer. Most of the time, it won't "feel" perfect or life changing. There will be unexpected interruptions, dryness, distractions, and other things that interfere. You will experience seasons of both joy and struggle in prayer. After a prayer time, resist the temptation to evaluate "how it went." Just be faithful, and over time you will grow in your ability to pray and to follow the subtler promptings of the Spirit throughout your day.

Appendix C
ACTS: A Way to Pray Every Day

Catholic Tradition teaches that four topics should be part of our prayer. These help to put us in right relationship to God and others, and to order our minds to the reality of God. When summarized by the following words, an acronym for easy recall results.

Adoration

Praise God: "My soul makes its boast in the LORD; / let the afflicted hear and be glad./ O magnify the Lord with me, / and let us exalt his name together!" (Psalm 34:2-3).

Contrition

Ask God to enlighten your heart in the areas that need to grow: "A broken and contrite heart, O God, thou wilt not despise" (Psalm 51:17).

Thanksgiving

The practice of gratitude fends off resentment and other poisonous states of mind: "It is good to give thanks to the LORD / . . . to declare thy steadfast love in the morning, / and thy faithfulness by night" (Psalm 92:1, 2).

Supplication

Petition; ask God for help: "Ask, and it will be given you. . . . For every one who asks receives" (Matthew 7:7-8).

You can spend a prayer time utilizing all four types, or pray each of the four separately in the day. For example, sing a song of praise on your walk to school or drive to work (A). Before you go to sleep, think about ways you fell short of love and ask for mercy and conversion (C). Give simple thanks to God for your meals and the good things that happened in the day (T). Ask for your needs and God's grace in the morning (S).

One of the simplest ways to grow in prayer is to spend two minutes on each letter of ACTS at some time every day, ideally the morning. If praising God (adoration) with words is unfamiliar, sing songs you like from a hymnal, or sing the Gloria or the Holy, Holy, Holy (*Sanctus*) from Mass. The psalms of praise are particularly useful to help us learn the language of giving God glory because God IS good.

Appendix D
A Guide to the Sacrament of Reconciliation

If it has been a long time since you last went to Confession—or if you've never been—you may be hesitant and unsure. Don't let these very common feelings get in your way. Reconciling with God and the Church always brings great joy. Take the plunge—you will be glad you did!

If it will help to alleviate your fears, familiarize yourself with the step-by-step description of the process below. Most priests are happy to help anyone willing to take the risk. If you forget anything, the priest will remind you. So don't worry about committing every step and word to memory. Remember, Jesus isn't giving you a test; he just wants you to experience the grace of his mercy!

Catholics believe that the priest acts *in persona Christi*, "in the person of Christ." The beauty of the sacraments is that they touch us both physically and spiritually. On the physical level in Confession, we hear the words of absolution through the person of the priest. On the spiritual level, we know that it is Christ assuring us that he has truly forgiven us. We are made clean!

You usually have the option of going to Confession anonymously—in a confessional booth or in a room with a screen—or face-to-face with the priest. Whatever you prefer will be fine with the priest.

Steps in the Sacrament of Reconciliation

1. Prepare to receive the sacrament by praying and examining your conscience. If you need help, you

can find many different lists of questions online that will help you examine your conscience.

2. Once you're with the priest, begin by making the Sign of the Cross while greeting the priest with these words: "Bless me, Father, for I have sinned." Then tell him how long it has been since your last confession. If it's your first confession, tell him so.

3. Confess your sins to the priest. If you are unsure about anything, ask him to help you. Place your trust in God, who is a merciful and loving Father.

4. When you are finished, indicate this by saying, "I am sorry for these and all of my sins." Don't worry later that you forgot something. This closing statement covers everything that didn't come to mind in the moment. Trust God that he has brought to mind what he wants you to address.

5. The priest will assign you a penance, such as a prayer, a Scripture reading, or a work of mercy, service, or sacrifice.

6. Express sorrow for your sins by saying an Act of Contrition. The following is one traditional Act of Contrition you may use. Many other versions can be found online, or you may simply say you're sorry in your words.

Act of Contrition:

My God, I am sorry for my sins with all my heart. In choosing to do wrong and failing to do good, I have sinned against you whom I should love above all things. I firmly intend, with your help, to do penance, to sin no more, and to avoid whatever leads me to sin. Our Savior Jesus Christ suffered and died for us. In his name, my God, have mercy.

7. The priest, acting in the person of Christ, will absolve you of your sins with prayerful words, ending with "I absolve you from your sins in the name of the Father, and of the Son, and of the Holy Spirit." You respond by making the Sign of the Cross and saying, "Amen."

8. The priest will offer some proclamation of praise, such as "Give thanks to the Lord, for he is good" (Psalm 136:1). You can respond, "His mercy endures forever."

9. The priest will dismiss you.

10. Be sure to complete your assigned penance immediately or as soon as possible.

APPENDICES

For Facilitators

E. The Role of a Facilitator

F. A Guide to Each Session of The Way

G. Leading Prayer and "Encountering Christ This Week"

Appendix E
The Role of the Facilitator

Perhaps no skill is more important to the success of a small group than the ability to facilitate a discussion lovingly. It is God's Holy Spirit working through our personal spiritual journey, not necessarily our theological knowledge, that makes this possible.

The following guidelines can help facilitators avoid some of the common pitfalls of small group discussion. The goal is to open the door for the Spirit to take the lead and guide your every response because you are attuned to his movements.

Pray daily and before your small group meeting. This is the only way you can learn to sense the Spirit's gentle promptings when they come!

You Are a Facilitator, Not a Teacher

As a facilitator, it can be extremely tempting to answer every question. You may have excellent answers and be excited about sharing them with your brothers and sisters in Christ. However, a more Socratic method, by which you attempt to draw answers from participants, is much more fruitful for everyone else and for you as well.

Get in the habit of reflecting participants' questions or comments to the whole group before offering your own input. It is not necessary for you as a facilitator to enter immediately into the discussion or to offer a magisterial answer. When others have sufficiently addressed an issue, try to exercise restraint in your comments. Simply affirm what has been said; then thank them and move on.

If you don't know the answer to a question, have a participant look it up in the *Catechism of the Catholic Church* and read it aloud to the group. If you cannot find an answer, ask someone to research the question for the next session. Never feel embarrassed to say, "I don't know." Simply acknowledge the quality of the question and offer to follow up with that person after you have done some digging. Remember, you are a facilitator, not a teacher.

Affirm and Encourage

We are more likely to repeat a behavior when it is openly encouraged. If you want more active participation and sharing, give positive affirmation to the responses of the group members. This is especially important if people are sharing from their hearts. A simple "Thank you for sharing that" can go a long way in encouraging further discussion in your small group.

If someone has offered a theologically questionable response, don't be nervous or combative. Wait until others have offered their input. It is very likely that someone will proffer a more helpful response, which you can affirm by saying something such as "That is the Christian perspective on that topic. Thank you."

If no acceptable response is given and you know the answer, exercise great care and respect in your comments so as not to appear smug or self-righteous. You might begin with something such as "Those are all interesting perspectives. What the Church has said about this is . . . "

Avoid Unhelpful Tangents

Nothing can derail a Spirit-filled discussion more quickly than digressing on unnecessary tangents. Try to keep the session on track. If conversation strays from the topic, ask yourself, "Is this a Spirit-guided tangent?" Ask the Holy Spirit too! If not, bring the group back by asking a question that steers conversation to the Scripture passage or to a question you have been discussing. You may even suggest kindly, "Have we gotten a little off topic?" Most participants will respond positively and get back on track through your sensitive leading.

That being said, some tangents may be worth pursuing if you sense a movement of the Spirit. It may be exactly where God wants to steer the discussion. You will find that taking risks can yield some beautiful results.

Don't Fear the Silence

Be okay with silence. Most people need a moment or two to come up with a response to a question. People naturally require some time to formulate their thoughts and put them into words. Some may need a few moments just to gather the courage to speak at all.

Regardless of the reason, don't be afraid of a brief moment of silence after asking a question. Let everyone in the group know early on that silence is an integral part of normal small group discussion. They needn't be anxious or uncomfortable when it happens. God works in silence!

This applies to times of prayer as well. If no one shares or prays after a sufficient amount of time, just move on gracefully.

The Power of Hospitality

A little hospitality can go far in creating community. Everyone likes to feel cared for. This is especially true in a small group whose purpose it is to connect to Jesus Christ, a model for care, support, and compassion.

Make a point to greet people personally when they first arrive. Ask them how their day has been going. Take some time to invest in the lives of your small group participants. Pay particular attention to newcomers. Work at remembering each person's name. Help everyone feel comfortable and at home. Allow your small group to be an environment in which authentic relationships take shape and blossom.

Encourage Participation

Help everyone to get involved, especially those who are naturally less vocal or outgoing. To encourage participation initially, always invite various group members to read aloud the selected readings. Down the road, even after the majority of the group feels comfortable sharing, you may still have some quieter members who rarely volunteer a response to a question but would be happy to read.

Meteorology?

Keep an eye on the "Holy Spirit barometer." Is the discussion pleasing to the Holy Spirit? Is this conversation leading participants to a deeper personal connection to Jesus Christ? The intellectual aspects of our faith are certainly important to discuss, but conversation can sometimes degenerate into an unedifying showcase of intellect and ego. Other times discussion becomes an opportunity for gossip, detraction, complaining, or even slander. When this happens, you can almost feel the Holy Spirit leaving the room!

If you are aware that this dynamic has taken over a discussion, take a moment to pray quietly in your heart. Ask the Holy Spirit to help you bring the conversation to a more wholesome topic. This can often be achieved simply by moving to the next question.

Pace

Generally, you want to pace the session to finish in the allotted time, but sometimes this may be impossible without sacrificing quality discussion. If you reach the end of your meeting and find that you have covered only half the material, don't fret! This is often the result of lively Spirit-filled discussion and meaningful theological reflection.

In such a case, you may take time at another meeting to cover the remainder of the material. If you have only a small portion left, you can ask participants to pray through these on their own and come to the following meeting with any questions or insights they may have. Even if you must skip a section to end on time, make sure you leave adequate time for prayer and to review the "Encountering Christ This Week" section. This is vital in helping participants integrate their discoveries from the group into their daily lives.

Genuine Friendships

The best way to show Jesus' love and interest in your small group members is to meet with them for coffee, dessert, or a meal outside of your small group time.

You can begin by suggesting that the whole group get together for ice cream or some other social event at a different time than when your group usually meets. Socializing will allow relationships to develop. It provides the opportunity for different kinds of conversations than small group sessions allow. You will notice an immediate difference in the quality of community in your small group at the next meeting.

After that first group social, try to meet one-on-one with each person in your small group. This allows for more in-depth conversation and personal sharing, giving you the chance to know each participant better so that you can love and care for them as Jesus would.

Jesus called the twelve apostles in order that they could "be with him" (Mark 3:14). When people spend time together, eat together, laugh together, cry together, and talk about what matters to them, intense Christian community develops. That is the kind of community Jesus was trying to create, and that must be the kind of community we try to create, because it changes lives. And changed lives change the world!

Joy

Remember that seeking the face of the Lord brings joy! Nothing is more fulfilling, more illuminating, and more beautiful than fostering a deep and enduring relationship with Jesus Christ. Embrace your participants and the entire spiritual journey with a spirit of joyful anticipation of what God wants to accomplish.

"These things I have spoken to you, that my joy may be in you, and that your joy may be full."
John 15:11

Appendix F
A Guide to Each Session of *The Way*

Session 1: Friendship with Jesus

If this is the first meeting of your small group, spend a few minutes facilitating introductions. Ask people to introduce themselves and share one other thing about themselves. The tone of the question should be light and nonreligious. For example, if the group is beginning in the fall, you could ask what was their favorite experience or memory from this past summer. You could ask about favorite sports teams or players, favorite movies or books, and why, and so forth. Avoid anything deeply personal. Your goal is to help people become comfortable before plunging into more substantive discussion.

Opening Prayer

For this first meeting, it would be ideal to pray a short, simple extemporaneous prayer before, after, or in lieu of the written prayer by St. Anselm. In your own words, ask God to bless your time together at this meeting and through the coming weeks. Ask God to make the meetings fruitful for everyone present.

Session Content

As explained in the introduction, the topics are arranged in two-week sets. The first week introduces a theme, and the second week continues and deepens the discussion on that theme. Thus, session 1, "Friendship with Jesus," is only the beginning of discussing the topic. In fact, the Scripture passage that explicitly references friendship ("No longer do I call you servants, . . . but I have called you friends," John 15:15) does not appear until session 2. Session 1 draws on people's experience of human friendship and deliberately provokes some contrast between the familiarity and ease we can feel in close friendships and the awe, even fear, we might fight feel in the presence of an all-powerful God. The Colossians reading attests to the divinity, power, and majesty of Jesus, inviting people into this mysterious and beautiful question of what it means to be friends of the living God. The passage from Pope Benedict XVI names what might be some common fears, and also proclaims some bold and reassuring truths regarding our faith in Jesus.

The goal of this discussion is not to teach or define exactly what friendship with Jesus should look or feel like, but to encourage a greater hunger and quest among participants to explore this for themselves. We hope to prompt genuine sharing about experiences, questions, fears, joys, and hopes. If the discussion gets too abstract or heady for very long, bring it back by asking questions about people's lived experiences of Jesus.

It may help to keep in mind that friendship with Jesus, who is both fully God and fully human at the same time, contains both similarities and differences when compared to human friendship. Also, people in the group may be in vastly different places regarding their experiences of God, prayer, and their consciousness of Jesus' enduring presence among them in the Holy Spirit. This session's discussion merely opens the door to a more explicit search. It is our hope that the rest of the sessions in *The Way,* parts 1 and 2 will aid each person in the process of seeking and finding their deepest longings in the love of Jesus Christ.[34]

---

[34] For a wonderful and formative supplement to this topic of friendship, listen to the free podcast *Spiritual Batteries* by Fr. Justin Gillespie, episode entitled "Friendship and Jesus," released on April 17, 2018.

Session 2: Jesus: True Source of Life

The Scripture passage for discussion this week (John 15:1-15) has a lot in it. Do not try to "cover" everything; remember, this is not a class! Prayerfully prepare to facilitate a Spirit-filled discussion with the questions provided, the notes below, and, most important, your own encounter with the Lord through this passage. As you prepare, remember also to pray for each member of your group by name, even if briefly.

A few notes may prove helpful in preparing for your discussion:

- Jesus is speaking to the eleven apostles in a discourse immediately following Judas' departure in John 13:30.

- The people of Israel are at times compared to a vine in the Old Testament, but one that has failed to bear the fruit God appointed them to bear. "I planted you a choice vine, / wholly of pure seed. / How then have you turned degenerate / and become a wild vine?" (Jeremiah 2:21; see also Isaiah 5:1-7, Ezekiel 19:10-14, and Psalm 80:8-15).[35] Jesus came to fulfill the vocation of Israel to truly be the vine that would bear the fruit of God's will, and in him, we too can participate in his fruitfulness.

- It may help to think of a common theme running through this passage as "attachment" or "dependency." The only true and worthy source of our full attachment, dependency, and trust is Jesus. By abiding in Jesus, we open ourselves to the Father's loving care, which nourishes and sustains us, gently pruning away our unhealthy attachments over

---

[35] Leo Zanchettin, ed., *John: A Devotional Commentary* (Frederick, Maryland: The Word Among Us, 2000), 166.

time, that we may grow stronger and bear more fruit of goodness in the world.

- See also Jesus' words earlier in this gospel: "All that the Father gives me will come to me; and him who comes to me I will not cast out" (John 6:37).

- Pay attention to the following words and how they are all connected: abide, love, joy, friends, commandments, fruit.

Finally, John 15:6 might stand out to some people as a harsh threat, or could even raise explicit questions about whether Jesus was referring to hell. Note that abstract discussions about hell and exactly how judgment works are often not very helpful in this small group setting. It's a topic that is hampered by our limited understanding and by a tendency to draw out strong emotions, overspeculation, and less-than-theologically accurate statements. All of this can lead to tension or an unhealthy discomfort among the group. Not all discomfort is bad, of course, for the Word of God will nudge and challenge us all in important ways. If you need to refocus the group in a more fruitful direction, however, invite them to call to mind the image of any gardener or "vinedresser" (15:1) tending to the care of plants. Notice how much patience, tenderness, love, and care go into gardening. It is not a rushed or harsh process, but a delicate and beautiful art. And the gardener delights to help the plants at every stage of their growth.

Thankfully, there are so many other powerful phrases in this passage, that it will not be hard to redirect the conversation if needed. For example, "Those are some great questions, Chris, and this matter has been debated among scholars for centuries. Let's return to discussing how the Lord's words speak to us about our daily lives. What do you all think: what are some practical ways we can abide in Jesus?"

Session 3: Prayer

This week's session directly opens up the all-important topic of prayer. Prayer, in one of its broadest definitions, is "the raising of one's mind and heart to God."[36] Prayer is about two-way communication between humans and God. This communication is both verbal and nonverbal; it is both communal and personal, and it can take about as many shapes and sizes as there are people. The sacraments are the most privileged, perfect, and potent prayers and means of prayer, and yet the prayerful life of an individual can be fostered in many ways, every day, and throughout the day. Individual personal prayer prepares the heart to better pray with the sacraments and to receive God's grace more fruitfully in an abundance of ways—in community, in liturgy, in God's word, in the poor, in conscience, in nature, and anywhere else the Lord wishes to reveal himself to us.

Sessions 3 and 4 both aim to inspire Spirit-filled discussions on this most sacred and mysterious aspect of our lives. Many people who pray or want to pray experience prayer as both a good thing and yet a struggle or a mystery they don't know how to enter into very deeply. This is a beautiful and holy struggle we hope to draw more people into through every session of *The Way*, but especially here in sessions 3 and 4. Sharing both joys and struggles regarding prayer is crucial for helping one another persevere and grow.

A few notes that might help in discussing the passage from Luke 11 are as follows:

- Importunity means persistence and perseverance.

- Be careful not to conclude from verse 8 that God is annoyed with us! A quick reading of the story might suggest as much, since the friend in the parable

---

[36] St. John Damascene, quoted in the *Catechism of the Catholic Church*, 2559.

just wants the guy to leave him alone! But the contrast running throughout the passage is between "you who are evil" (verse 13) and the perfect, loving, heavenly Father. We imperfect lovers are often motivated to help others by less-than-perfect motives (like avoiding inconvenience to ourselves), and yet even we still do what is right and good quite often; how much more, then, can our perfect heavenly Father always be trusted to do what is right and good!

- If anyone is bothered by the line "you who are evil," it might help to remind them that the broader revelation of both Scripture and Church Tradition radically affirms that we are made in God's image and our substance (along with all of creation) is "very good" (Genesis 1:31). At the same time, however, we are sinners in need of a savior; even as Christians who say yes to Jesus the Savior, we participate in evil (sin), and our salvation, healing, and growth in Christ are not yet fully complete. "You who are evil" is a contrast between we who are being saved and God who is the all-good Savior.

- Adoration of the Father (acknowledging God's goodness and praising him) is the first part of the Lord's prayer, as this practice properly situates our concerns, which we are then to bring to him.

- See *Catechism*, 2613 on St. Luke's three parables on prayer for further optional background reading.

Closing Prayer

Given that this week's topic is prayer, it's an especially appropriate week to spend some extra time in prayer together as a group. If you have time, you might read the selection by Peter Kreeft found in "Encountering Christ This Week" as a lead-in to your closing prayer time. Use Kreeft's words as an invitation to members to use their own words in your group prayer time and not to worry about sounding profound or eloquent. For a helpful method in encouraging deeper shared prayer together, see the Sticky Note Prayer at the end of the notes for session 6 below (on page 97).

Session 4: A Habit of Prayer

This second week on prayer is connected to the first (session 3) in a number of ways. Not only does it continue with the same topic, but the Scripture reading specifically addresses "anxiety," which you began discussing in the beginning of session 3. The Pope Benedict XVI selection (from *Jesus of Nazareth*) also comments further on passages discussed last week. Before reading each passage, you might wish to point these connections out, or you could wait until a discussion has occurred for a bit and then see if anyone recalls any points or questions from last week that are further illumined by this week's passages. This kind of recollection and repetition can be helpful for learning, retention, and application to life.

When discussing Philippians 4:4-9, help the group pay attention to just how *practical* this passage really is. "Have no anxiety" is not something we can just do or make happen on our own, and of course there's no magic formula for avoiding it. Paul's words might sound a little trite or even offensive, especially for people who have suffered deeply from ailments like anxiety disorder and depression. This discussion is not the time to dive into the genuine complexities of mental health and psychology. Yet there is some very practical wisdom to gain from this passage for how to respond to common, daily worries, anxieties, and stresses. Try to draw people into these practical considerations and ask what they might look like in practice. For example,

- Worry, stress, and anxiety are an invitation to bring one's concerns to the Lord in prayer.

- What does this mean to "rejoice always"? Are Paul's words in verse 4 just a nice-sounding throw-away line? Or are there practices that can help us cultivate a joyful heart? For example, you might dedicate five minutes an evening to reflect back on your day and try to find at least one thing worth rejoicing over. For a list of the types of things to rejoice over, see verse 8. A practice like this helps build a habit of looking for, recognizing, and re-sponding to God's goodness in our lives.

- Similarly, "with thanksgiving" is a key ingredient even in "making your requests known to God" (verse 6). When asking God for help (which we're instructed—even commanded—to do), find some-thing in that request to be thankful for. If you're having a struggle with your child, first, thank God for the gift of this child and the privilege of partner-ing with God to form and raise them. Or if you're stressed about a situation at work, first consider how grateful you are for the employment. Identify and voice that thanksgiving, and then move onto the request.

- Third, "let your requests be made known to God." This harkens back to last week's passage on persistence. Note the strangeness of the wording: how can we make something known to God, who knows all things? Of course, God already knows what we want and need, but he speaks to us like a loving Father once again through the inspired words of St. Paul here. "Let your requests be made known to God," as you would to a loving parent or close friend. Relationships are built upon and strengthened by this kind of trusting communication. Sharing our hearts and concerns might not add knowledge to God, but it certainly can open the pathways of our hearts to greater intimacy and trust in the Lord.

- Finally, verse 8 is a powerful and practical list of the types of things to deliberately think about in prayer and in life. How do people in the group do this? How do you? What are some new ways you could try to strengthen a habit of "think[ing] about these things"?

Encountering Christ This Week

There are two parts to this week's material for reflection and prayer at home. The first encourages a greater habit of prayer and the second encourages participation in daily Mass and/or the Sacrament of Reconciliation. *The Way, Part 2* contains sessions and supporting material on the Eucharist and Reconciliation, but we need not wait for those weeks to be reminded of the importance of the sacraments in our prayer lives. As you point out the "Encountering Christ This Week" content to people this week, perhaps provide a very brief witness to the beauty and power of the Sacrament of Reconciliation in your life. Also let people know of some local Confession times at or around your parish/community.

Closing Prayer

If you did not use the Sticky Note Prayer method last week, perhaps try it out this week. See instructions at the end of the notes for session 6 on page 97. If you did use it last week and it was well received, consider doing it again and possibly adding the layer of step 5. Either way, try to lead a more extended group prayer time of at least ten minutes.

Session 5: Sacred Scripture

While Scripture is the primary source of reflection for every session of *The Way,* this week begins the first of two sessions reflecting directly on the role and power of Scripture in our lives as disciples.

As usual, the discussion questions should open up some honest personal sharing and will touch on some weighty theological principles. Try to keep the discussion moving in a direction of personal experience and application regarding the power of Scripture to speak to us. Seek to open up the wondrous mystery that God has chosen to communicate to us in such a tangible way as through written words. When we approach those words in humility and openness, in prayer, and with the guidance of the Church, we are in a privileged place of encountering the One who inspired them.

Doctrinal explanations and perfect clarity on a theology of revelation are not the goal of this session, but the following notes and references may help you know when to redirect the conversation or to point people to further research if needed.

We believe that "all scripture is inspired by God" (2 Timothy 3:16). But what does this mean? The Church's understanding of biblical inspiration can first be understood from a number of statements about what we do *not* believe.

The Bible is *not*

- merely a human text,

- dictated word-for-word by God to humans acting as mere puppets,

- the only source of knowing truth, or

- an answer manual addressing every possible topic of human inquiry.

Biblical inspiration is an inspired interworking of grace and human freedom. "God is its principal author, with the writer as the human collaborator. Thus the Scriptures are the word of God in human language."[37]

The Church helps us avoid error by giving us principles for scriptural interpretation.[38] We could summarize these principles by saying that we do not only read a line or book of Scripture in isolation and try to grasp its full meaning. While we believe God can speak to us through any line of Scripture, and while prayerful encounters with the Bible are available for all believers, the fullness of a text's meaning emerges when understood in connection with the entire Bible and the Tradition of the Church. This is why it is helpful to occasionally consult the footnotes in a Catholic Bible and the *Catechism of the Catholic Church* in both our small groups and our personal study.

In this week's session, the Vatican II selection from *Dei Verbum* mentions Sacred Tradition, sometimes referred to as Apos-

---

[37] Footnote to 2 Timothy 3:16 in *New American Bible Revised Edition*.

[38] See the three basic principles in the *Catechism*, 112–114.

tolic Tradition. See the following selection from the *Compendium of the Catechism of the Catholic Church* if clarity is needed.[39]

12. What is Apostolic Tradition?

Apostolic Tradition is the transmission of the message of Christ, brought about from the very beginnings of Christianity by means of preaching, bearing witness, institutions, worship, and inspired writings. The apostles transmitted all they received from Christ and learned from the Holy Spirit to their successors, the bishops, and through them to all generations until the end of the world. (See *Catechism*, 75–79, 83, 96, 98.)

13. In what ways does Apostolic Tradition occur?

Apostolic Tradition occurs in two ways: through the living transmission of the word of God (also simply called Tradition) and through Sacred Scripture which is the same proclamation of salvation in written form. (See *Catechism*, 76.)

14. What is the relationship between Tradition and Sacred Scripture?

Tradition and Sacred Scripture are bound closely together and communicate one with the other. Each of them makes present and fruitful in the Church the mystery of Christ. They flow out of the same divine wellspring and together make up one sacred deposit of faith from which the Church derives her certainty about revelation. (See *Catechism*, 80–82, 97.)

---

[39] http://www.vatican.va/archive/compendium_ccc/documents/archive_2005_compendium-ccc_en.html

Session 6: Reactions to the Word of God

This week's session provides a wonderfully rich Scripture passage for personal reflection and sharing—the parable of the sower and the seed. Note that this parable refers to the seeds as "the word," which has several meanings, not limited only to the Bible. Most broadly "the word" refers to the good news of God's kingdom, which Jesus preached about and opened up for us to live in, in a new way, even here on earth. Jesus himself is "the Word made flesh" (*Catechism,* 475, see also John 1:1-18). The four categories of the types of soil provide a helpful metaphor for sharing about our experiences of receiving the good news of Jesus, and our common struggles to allow that word to transform us and bear fruit.

As you discuss the sower and the seed and as you bring these initial six sessions of *The Way* to a close, pay particular attention to ensure that the trajectory of the conversation points towards personal application. As Pope Francis said well, a common temptation when listening to God's word is "to think about what the text means for other people, and so avoid applying it to our own life."[40] To help you with this, make a particular effort to end by spending sufficient time on the final question. You may or may not need to ask question 5, depending on how much conversation ensued before that. If you have time and want to keep digging, ask question 5; if you're running out of time, move on to question 6. Just don't skip question 6! Leave at least 15 minutes for closing reflections and prayer after the discussion of Scripture.

---

[40] Pope Francis, Apostolic Exhortation *Evangelii Gaudium*, November 24, 2013, 153, http://w2.vatican.va/content/francesco/en/apost_exhortations/documents/papa-francesco_esortazi-one-ap_20131124_evangelii-gaudium.html.

One-on-One Follow-Up

As people share their responses to the kinds of soil their hearts currently represent, be especially aware of comments that indicate someone's openness to deeper interior conversion to Jesus. This could be a privileged moment or season of deepening conversion in someone's life in your group! In the week following this session, could you personally reach out to and follow up with at least one person from your group who seems most hungry for more growth? Ask them to get together to hear more of their story, continue the conversations this resource has opened up, and pray with them.

Closing Prayer and What's Next

Prior to closing in prayer, invite the group members to reflect back on the six-week journey you just shared together through *The Way, Part 1*. What have they experienced? Is there any session or topic that stands out the most to them? Is there anything in particular that is most memorable or meaningful for them? Pausing to ask and answer questions like these is a wonderful way to solidify and spread some of the graces experienced. In your closing prayer time, make sure to offer some extemporaneous prayers of gratitude for the entire six-session journey you just traveled together. Perhaps also facilitate the Sticky Note Prayer method (again or for the first time); see below for instructions.

We hope that these six sessions of *The Way, Part 1* not only blessed your group's time together with inspiring and transformative conversations, but also that they whet their appetite to complete *The Way, Part 2*. Propose continuing right away or after taking a break. You may wish to organize a social or service outing between now and when your group begins the next resource.

Sticky Note Prayer: A Method for Group Prayer

Allow at least ten minutes.

1. Pass out a sticky note and pen to each person.

2. Instruct group members to write their name and a prayer intention on the sticky note. Especially encourage them to make it a prayer intention for themselves, not an intention for another person in their life. (What do you need God's help with right now?) Let them know they will be sharing these intentions with the group.

3. Invite each person to share aloud what they wrote. Tell people to listen to everyone, but to pay particular attention to the person on their right; as they'll be invited to pray for that person later.

4. After each person has shared about their prayer intention, instruct everyone to pass their note to the person on their left.

5. Invite the group to each pray aloud briefly, in succession, for the person on their right. If they need help remembering the person's prayer request, all they need to do is look at the sticky note in their hands. If you think it will help, you can suggest a simple formula they can follow to get started: "Jesus, thank you for ______. Please help him/her with ________ (what's on the note)." Note: If the group is not ready for this amount of extemporaneous prayer, you can pray extemporaneously for the group and skip the step of inviting them to each pray for someone. You can work in this step lat-

er, after doing the Sticky Note Prayer a few more weeks without it.

6. Encourage each person to take home the note they received as a reminder to pray for that person throughout the coming week.

7. Close with a traditional prayer all can say together.

Appendix G
Leading Prayer and
"Encountering Christ This Week"

Opening Prayer

We have provided a guided opening prayer for each session because it can help people who are completely new to small groups and shared extemporaneous prayer feel more at ease. If everyone or most people present are already comfortable speaking to God in their own words aloud in a group, you won't need these prayers at all. It's always better to talk to God from our hearts in a small group. It contributes to the intimacy of the group and also builds individual intimacy with God.

Since some people have never witnessed spontaneous prayer, it's part of your role to model it. Prayers from the heart spoken aloud demonstrate how to talk to God honestly and openly. Seeing someone pray this way expands a person's understanding of who God is and the relationship he or she can have with Jesus Christ.

You can grow in extemporaneous prayer by praying aloud directly to Jesus during your personal prayer time and as you prepare for the group. This will help "prime the pump," so to speak.

Even if you enjoy praying aloud spontaneously, your goal as a facilitator is to provide opportunities for everyone to grow spiritually. People who pray aloud with others grow by leaps and bounds—we've seen it! After the first meeting, tell the group that you will allow time at the end of your extemporaneous prayer for others to voice prayers. As soon as the group appears to have grown into this, invite other people to open the group with prayer instead of leading it yourself or using the prayer provided.

If you don't do it in the first meeting, in the second week, pray the opening prayer in your own words. Here are some simple parts to include:

1. Praise God! Say what a great and wonderful God our Father is. Borrow language from the psalms of praise if you don't have your own. Just search online for "praise psalms."

2. Thank God! Thank the Lord for the gift of gathering together. Thank him for giving each person present the desire to sacrifice their time to attend the group. Thank him for the blessing of your parish or campus community.

3. Ask God for your needs. Ask God to bless your time together and to make it fruitful for all present as well as for his kingdom. Ask Jesus to be with you, who are two or three gathered in his name. Ask the Holy Spirit to open hearts, illuminate minds, and deepen each person's experience through the Scripture passages you'll read and discuss. Ask the Holy Spirit to guide the discussion so that you can all grow from it.

4. Close by invoking Jesus: "We pray this through Christ our Lord" or "We pray this in Jesus' name."

5. End with the Sign of the Cross.

Some Essentials for Extemporaneous Prayer

- Speak in the first person plural "we." For example, "Holy Spirit, we ask you to open our hearts . . ." It's fine to add a line asking the Holy Spirit to help you facilitate the discussion as he wills or something else to that effect, but most of the prayer should be for the whole group.

- Model speaking directly to Jesus our Lord. This may sound obvious, but among Catholic laypeople, it isn't frequently practiced or modeled. This is a very evangelical thing to do in the sense that it witnesses to the gospel. Not only does it show how much we believe that the Lord loves us, but it also demonstrates our confidence that Jesus himself is listening to us! As we say our Lord's name, we remind ourselves, as well as those who hear us, that we aren't just talking to ourselves. This builds up faith.

- You and anyone unaccustomed to hearing someone pray to Jesus directly may feel a bit uncomfortable at first. But group members will quickly become more at ease as they hear these prayers repeatedly and experience more intimacy with Jesus. Bear in mind always that many graces come from praying "the name which is above every name" (Philippians 2:9).

- If you've never publicly prayed to Jesus, you may feel childish at first, but pray for the humility of a child. After all, Jesus did say that we needed to "become like children" (Matthew 18:3)! The more we pray directly to Jesus in our personal prayer, the less awkward it will feel when we pray to him publicly.

- Model great faith and trust that the Lord hears your prayer and will answer it. It's terrific just to say in prayer, "Jesus, we trust you!"

- You can always close extemporaneous prayer by inviting the whole group to join in a prayer of the Church, such as the Glory Be, the Our Father, or the Hail Mary. This will bring everyone into the prayer if previously, just one person was praying aloud extemporaneously.

Closing Prayer

For the closing prayer, we recommend that you always include extemporaneous prayer, even if you also use the prayer provided. No written prayer can address the thoughts, concerns, feelings, and inspirations that come up during the discussion. If some group members already feel comfortable praying aloud in their own words, invite the group to join in the closing prayer right away. If not, wait a week or two. Once you feel that the group has the familiarity to prevent this from being too awkward, invite them to participate. You could tell the group that you will begin the closing prayer and then allow for a time of silence so that they can also pray aloud. Make sure they know that you will close the group's prayer by leading them into an Our Father after everyone is done praying spontaneously. This structure helps people feel that the time is contained and not completely lacking in structure. That helps free them to pray aloud.

Below are some possible ways to introduce your group to oral extemporaneous prayer. Don't read these suggestions verbatim—put them into your own words. It's not conducive to helping people become comfortable praying aloud spontaneously if you are reading out of a book!

"The closing prayer is a great time to take the reflections we've shared, bring them to God, and ask him to help us make any inspirations a reality in our lives. God doesn't care about how well-spoken or articulate we are when we pray, so we shouldn't either! We don't judge each other's prayers. Let's just pray from our hearts, knowing that God hears and cares about what we say, not how perfectly we say it. When we pray something aloud, we know that the Holy Spirit is mightily at work within us because it's the Spirit who gives us the courage to speak."

"Tonight for the closing prayer, let's first each voice our needs to one another; then we will take turns praying for the person to the right of us. After we each express our prayer needs, I will start by praying for Karen on my right. That means that I need to listen carefully when she tells us what she needs prayer for. We may not remember everyone's needs, so be sure to listen well to the person on your right. I'll voice my prayer needs first; then we'll go around the circle to the right. Then I will begin with the Sign of the Cross and pray for Karen. Okay? Does anyone have any questions?"

For a method of group prayer that is particularly effective in helping people grow in comfort both with sharing prayer intentions and with praying for one another, see the Sticky Note Prayer method outlined at the end of appendix F on page 97.

Encountering Christ This Week

These weekly prayer and reflection exercises allow Jesus to enter more fully into the hearts of you and your small group members. If we don't give God the time that allows him to work in us, we experience far less fruit from our small group discussions. Prayer and reflection water the seeds that have been planted during the small group so that they can take root. Without the "water" of prayer and reflection, the sun will scorch the seed, and it will shrivel up and die, "since it had no root" (Mark 4:6). Encountering Christ during the week on our own makes it possible for us to be "rooted" in Christ (Colossians 2:7) and to drink deeply of the "living water" (John 4:10) that he longs to pour into our souls.

Please review the "Encountering Christ This Week" section in advance so that you're familiar with it, and then together as a group during each meeting. Reviewing it together will show everyone that it is an important part of the small group. Ask for feedback each week about how these prayer and reflection exercises are going. Don't spend too long on this topic, however, especially in the early weeks while members are still becoming comfortable together and growing more accustomed to praying on their own. Asking about their experience with the recommended prayer, sacrament, or spiritual exercise will help you know who is hungry for spiritual growth and who might need more encouragement. The witness of participants' stories from their times of prayer can ignite the interest of others who are less motivated to pray.